More PLEXERS™

By

Dave Hammond
Tom Lester
Joe Scales

DALE
SEYMOUR
PUBLICATIONS
P.O. BOX 10888
PALO ALTO, CA 94303

ACKNOWLEDGEMENTS

We would like to thank Mary Ann Maberry of the Sacramento Bee for her support and encouragement; Budd Westreich for his valuable suggestions and printing moxie; Greer Elementary School staff; teachers of the MICA Project; and students at California State University at Sacramento for their creative suggestions and ideas for several of the following Plexers.

Finally to our families, whose long-suffering involvement included creation of many of the original Plexers found in this volume.

Dave Hammond
Tom Lester
Joe Scales

INTRODUCTION

Plexers™* is derived from the word *perplex* which means "to make unable to grasp something clearly or to think logically and decisively about something." It is our goal with this book to encourage students to think logically and decisively.

Plexers are a type of rebus, or what we consider insight-phrases. They are usually words. (The general form of a rebus contains pictures as well as words.) Students are to determine what word or phrase the Plexer brings to mind. The direction, size and/or position of the letters are often vital to understanding the puzzle.

Plexers can help students develop some expertise in problem solving. They allow students to try different solutions without the pressure of being graded on their answer. Students can develop divergent thinking skills through taking the necessary different views of symbols and coding. The puzzles often have more than one possible solution. (Solutions other than those given in the answer section may even be better!)

We find it important that the teacher or other students who solve a Plexer first not give the answer to students still trying to solve the puzzle. We like everyone to have an opportunity to think about a Plexer. One thing we find in schools is the strong urge to always have CLOSURE. The important stage of problem solving, which we call the "incubation stage," is rarely allowed in classrooms. To leave problems open for an hour, a day, a week, etc., and first give students hints allows students time for incubation. Hints can often generate alternative thought sequences of those who have not solved the Plexer.

Using *More Plexers* in the classroom

1. Add a Plexer to a worksheet, quiz, or test as a last question or as a "fun" item.

2. Post 2-3 Plexers on the bulletin board. At a convenient time of the day, ask for hands on who has a conjecture of what the Plexer is. Very hard Plexers may stay on the board for a couple of days or more. Provide a new hint each day.

3. Give a copy of a page of Plexers to your students. Have them work individually, in pairs, or in small groups to solve the puzzles. Then let students tell how they solved the Plexers— the different thought processes they went through to reach their solutions. This could be developed into a class discussion on problem-solving techniques.

*Plexers is a registered trademark of Plexers, Inc.

4. Set up a Plexer box. Duplicate puzzles from this book and paste them on index cards. Write the solutions on the backs of the cards or make the solution key from this book available to the students. (Remember not to cut off the puzzle numbers!)

5. Give each student a different Plexer. Let the students solve it and then create their own Plexers for the same solution.

6. After your students have solved a few puzzles, they probably will be ready to create their own. Let the students create Plexers to be solved by their classmates. Students might post their puzzles on the bulletin board or might create a class "original Plexers" box.

Note: Be sure a box or border is always drawn around the Plexers; the box gives license to use spelling and grammatical errors that would not be acceptable in students' daily work.

1

$$D_E {}_A{}^{T\,H}$$

2

2nd ∅

3

AGE —

4

AALLLL

5

I'M 1,2,3
U

6

PEN
sword

7

G
HISTORY

8

B B B B
A A A A
R R R R
G G G G

9

U WIN +
U LOSE +

10

ICE

11

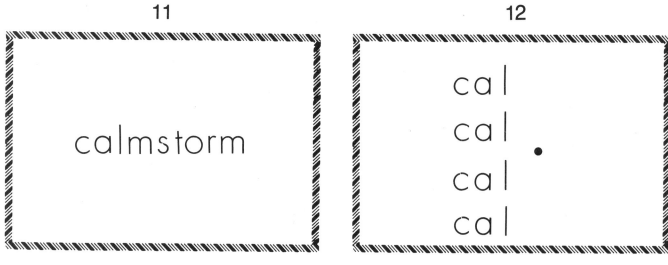

calmstorm

12

cal
cal .
cal
cal

13

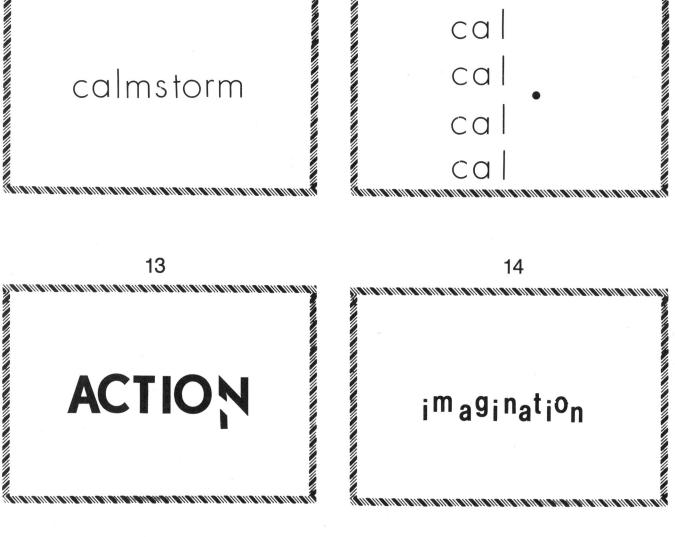

ACTION

14

imagination

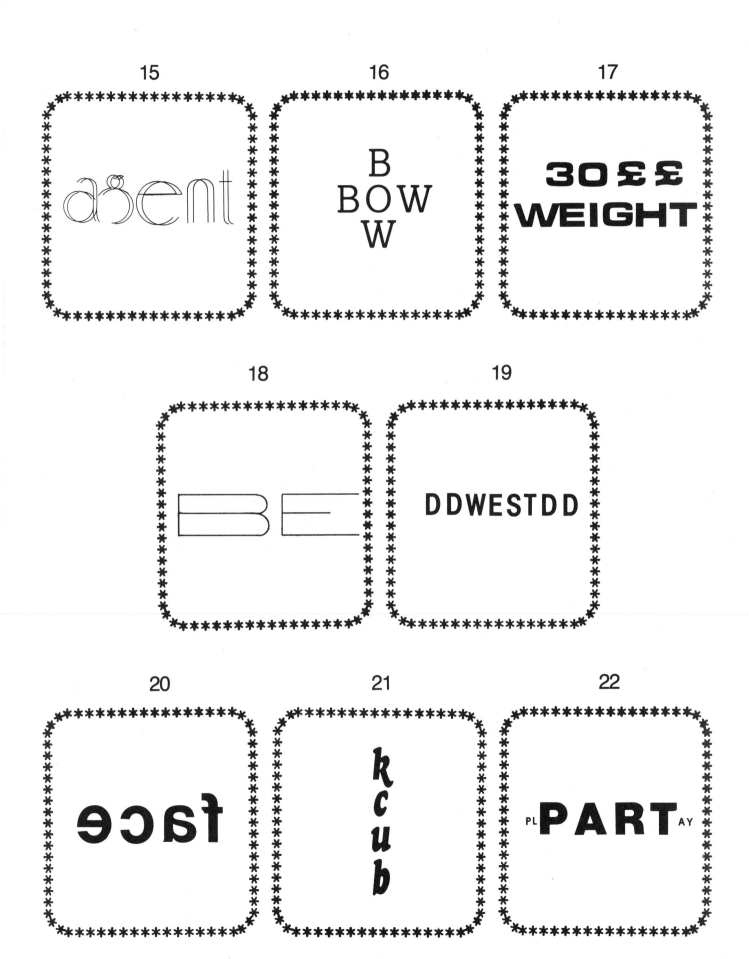

15

agent

16

B
BOW
W

17

WEIGHT

18

BE

19

DDWESTDD

20

face

21

k
c
u
b

22

PL PART AY

23

N
KEY   E
S

24

of the**wear**Green

25

Purpose
Purpose

26

AT FRANK RA
FRANK

27

— BELL

28

ESREV

29

ANTICIPATION

30

OT U

4

31

PLANE

32

BONBNET

33

$$e$$
$$c$$
$$n$$
$$o$$
$$a\ 4:37$$

34

FACRISISMILY

35

brain
brain
brain
brawn

36

ON
ROAD   ON
ROAD

37

GOING
55MPH

38

. ____

39

pflashan

40

AWL i|c| (circle above)

41

+VERB

42

LET^gone B^gone
  gone gone

43

YYUR
YYUB
I C U R
YY4ME

44

PpOpD

45

  O   K
R C Y

46

I ☐ ☐

47

bit **MORE**

48

GENE

49

**DICE
TROUBLE
DICE**

50

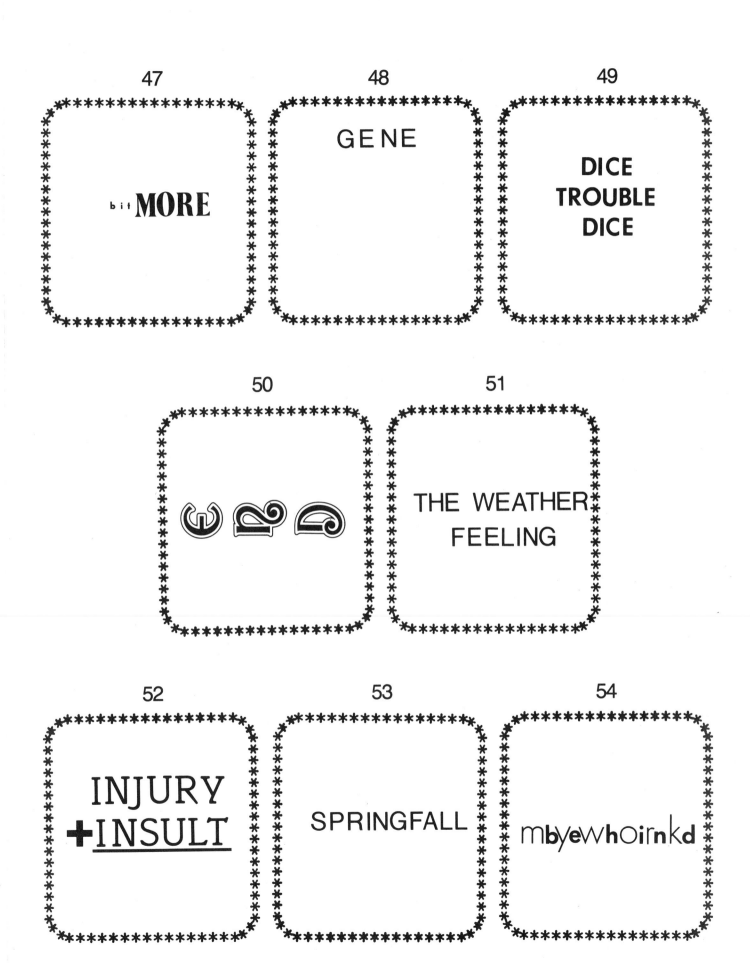

51

THE WEATHER
FEELING

52

**INJURY
+INSULT**

53

SPRINGFALL

54

mbyewhOirnkd

7

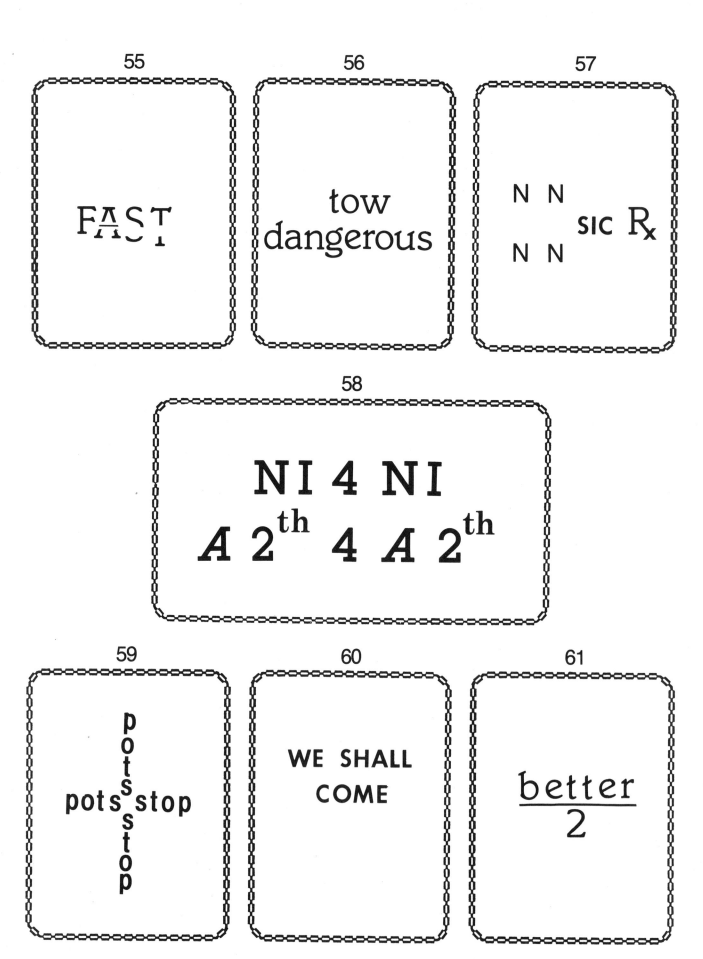

8

62

DENIM
AWLAWL

63

& x

64

M
U

65

t
a
ble

66

RAPIDS

67

idl

68

many love
many love

69

T the T
U U
B B
E E

70

nerve nerve

9

71

¢10 I A L

72

W
u A
P L
L
L

73

h   a

t

74

DICTATORSHIP
LIVING

75

bopper

76

burn °°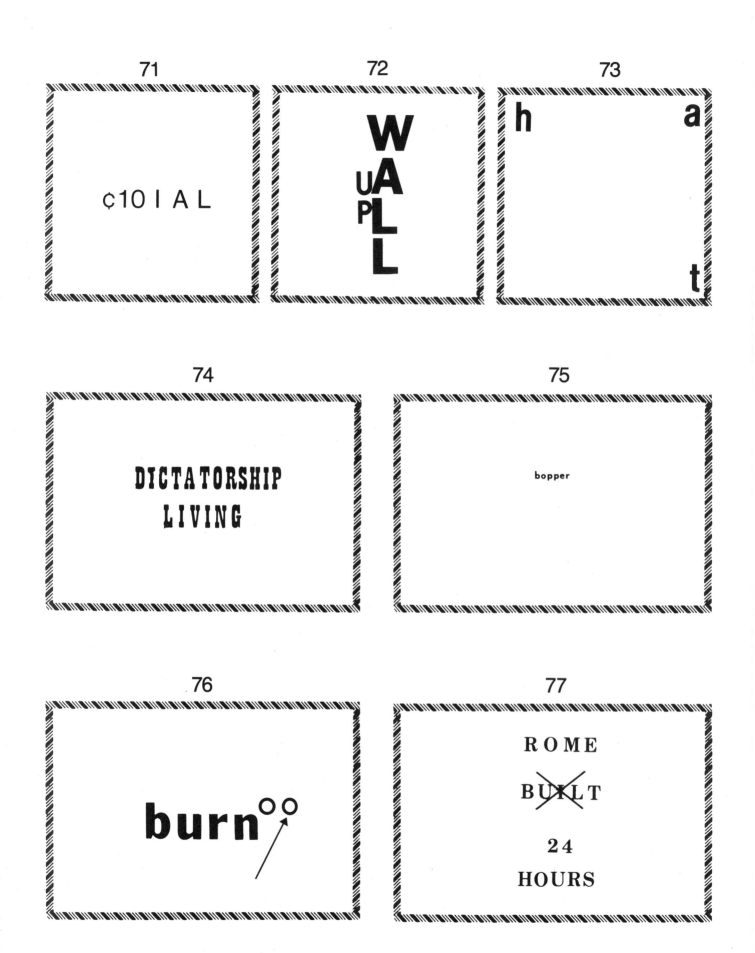

77

ROME
BU~~I~~LT
24
HOURS

78

C A N E

79

$\frac{L}{4}$

80

get
away
Ø

81

business pleasure

82

—PUNCH—

83

TREE

84

PAYMENT

85

E T H
R
A
T E

86

87

88

UUDAY

89

90

91

SULIFERANCE

92

WIRE
GETTING IN

93

MINUTE

94

D O O R

POLICY

95

lib
+lib

96

10 *1st*

97

annoyed
annoyed

98

S
C
A
L
E

99

thethe
Nth°

100

FIRE
TOUGH

101

in in in
in in

102

A.$^{t}_{g}$ early M.

103

O dom

104

IoRUve

105

play
B
T A
E S
K

106

MBRK
————
JOURNEY

107

SKY

SKY

108

cents
cents
cents
cents
cents
cents ←

HE HE

HI LL

C

place
3:46

delayed
―――――
1,2,3 rain

going

SO

S
E
M
I
T

LLAC

117

going
DIET

118

& dddd

119

M M
U U
S S

120

P   T
　L   I
　　I C
　　C I
　L   I
P   T

121

ZZZZ

122

WORK

HAHANDND

123

10ASUN

16

124

N 10S HEAT

125

F
I
N
E

126

JUST
+ JUST
───────

127

B
U
R
N

B
U
R
N

128

I   2th

$I \ 2^{th}$

129

SAgoingNE

130

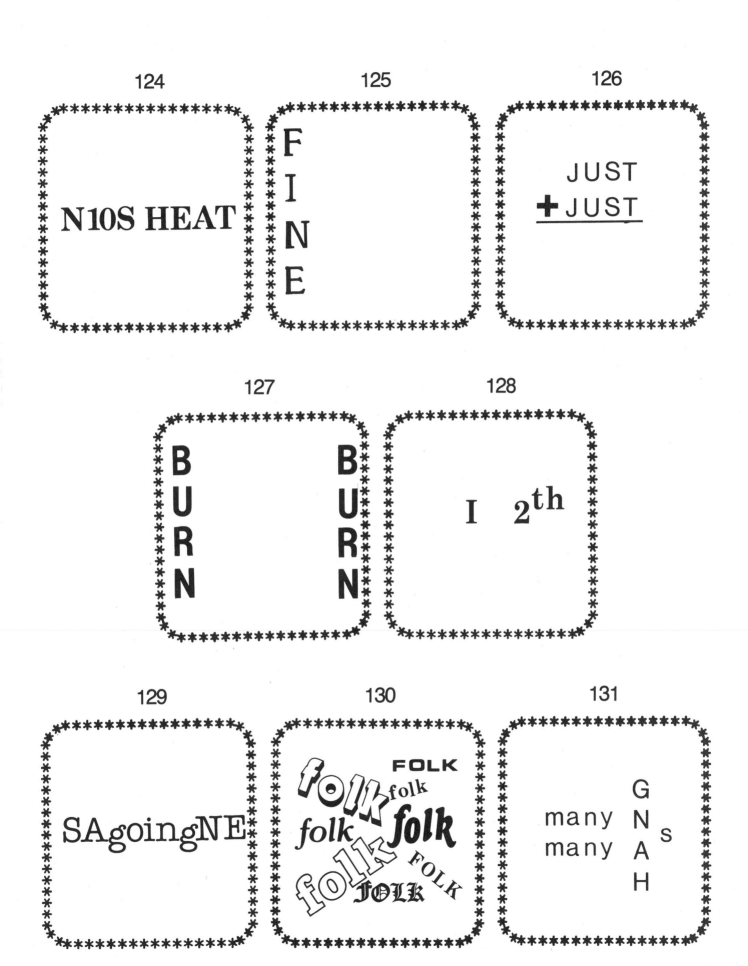

131

many   G
many   N
      A
      H   s

132

NEW LEAF *(inverted)*

133

2:47
ur hand
hand

134

= A T

135

NOMMAG

136

guay guay *(inverted)*

137

GO   E   OD
     K
MO   A   OD
     W

138

+ where
rainbow

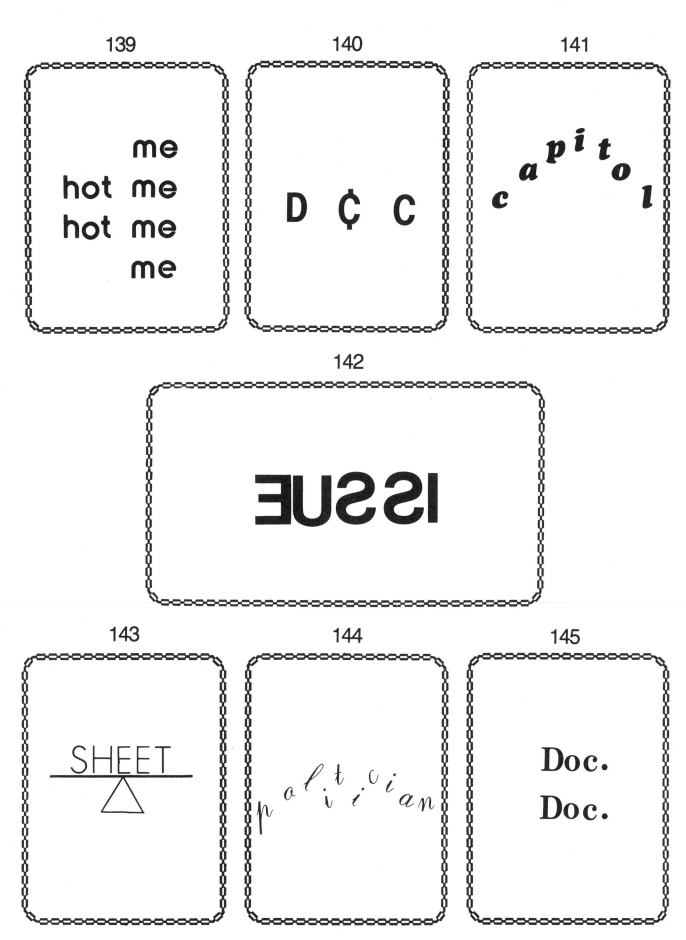

139

me
hot me
hot me
me

140

D ¢ C

141

c a p i t o l

142

ISSUE

143

SHEET
△

144

politician

145

Doc.
Doc.

feiengl
feiengl

NUTer

GOLD

Fe

Fe **old** Fe

Fe

tracked   tracked

GAawlME

coming   something

KET

E D I S   N   A N O T H E R

FADE

FINI   TIVE

DASHOTRK

FIRE
+ FUEL

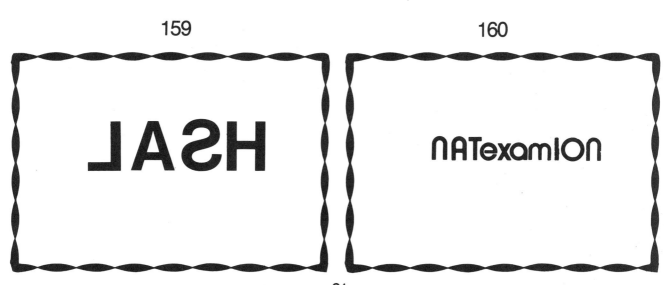

LASH

NATexamION

161

162

163

164

165

everyrightthing

166

COM £

167

STOP
10¢

168

SELL

BUY

169

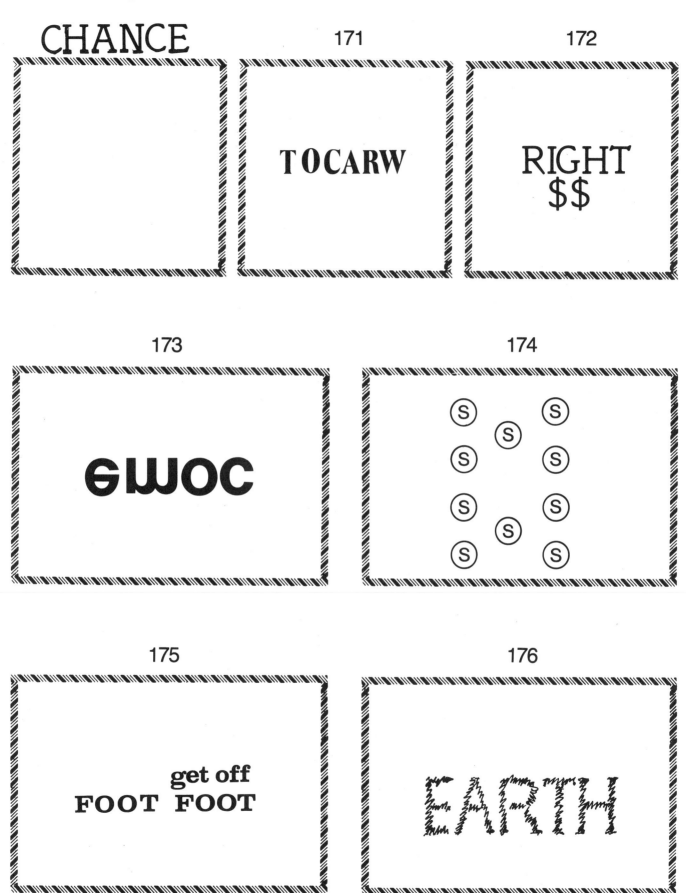

170

CHANCE

171

TOCARW

172

RIGHT
$$

173

GWOC

174

175

get off
FOOT FOOT

176

EARTH

23

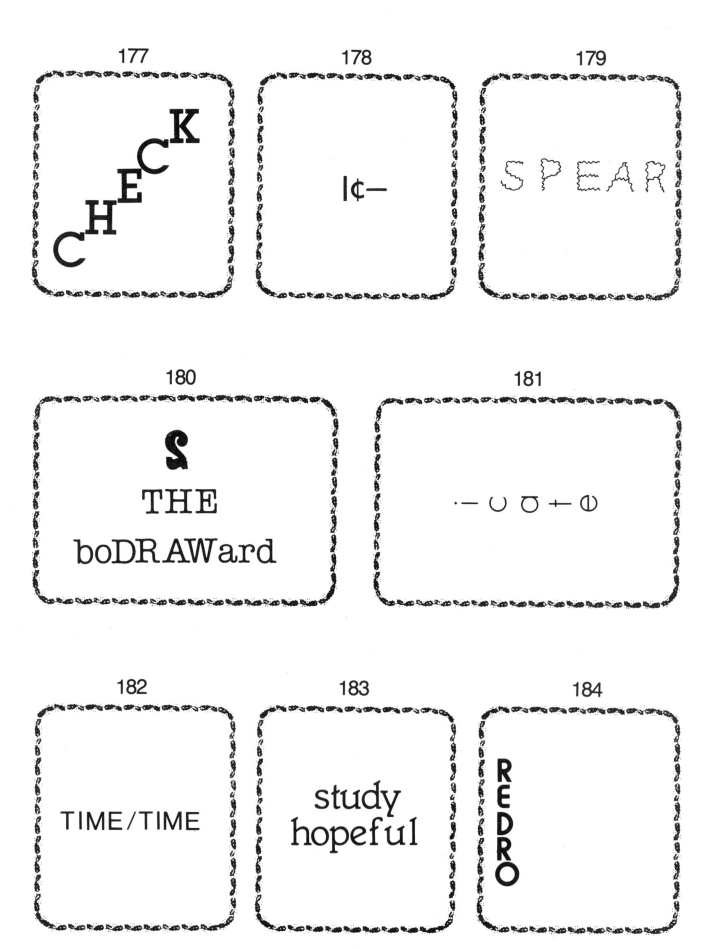

177

CHECK

178

I¢—

179

SPEAR

180

S
THE
boDRAWard

181

·—∪□+①

182

TIME/TIME

183

study
hopeful

184

REDRO

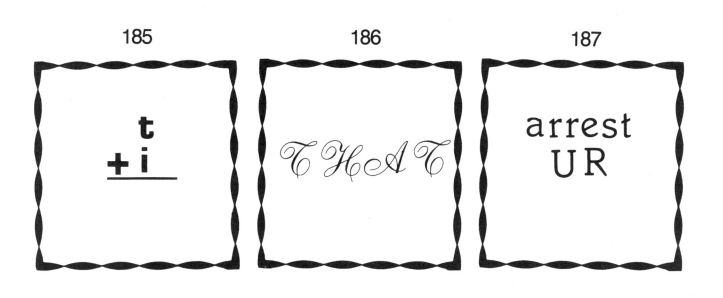

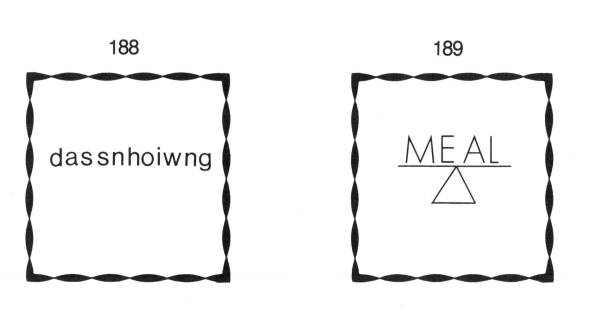

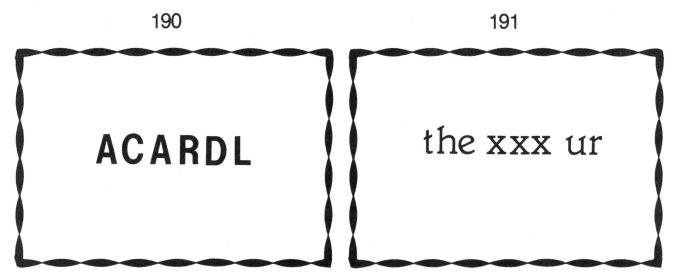

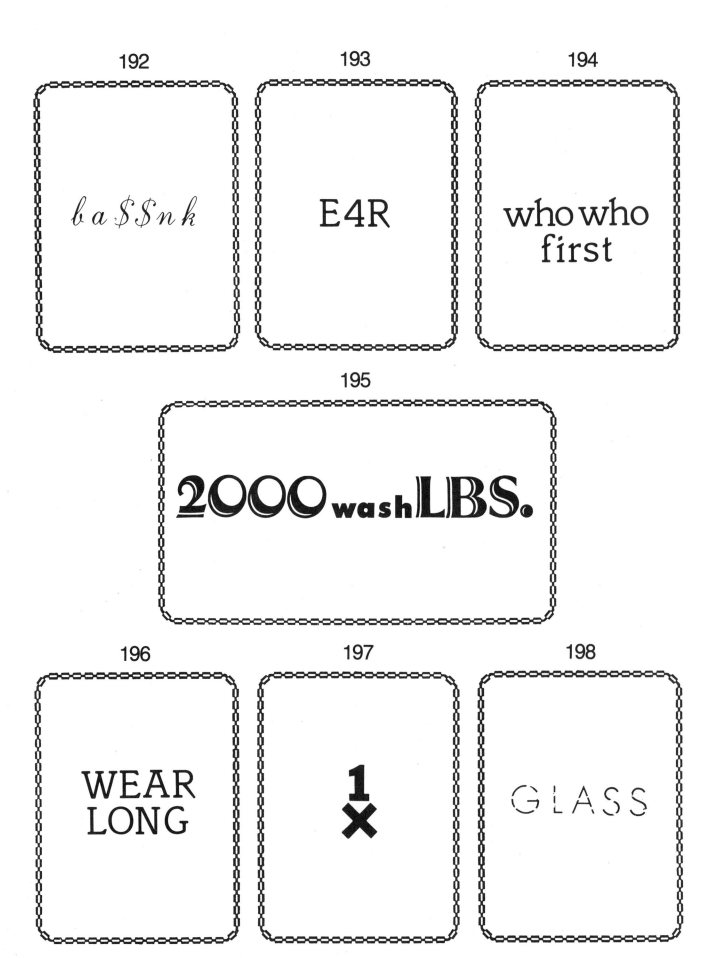

192

ba$$nk

193

E4R

194

who who
first

195

2000 wash LBS.

196

WEAR
LONG

197

1
X

198

GLASS

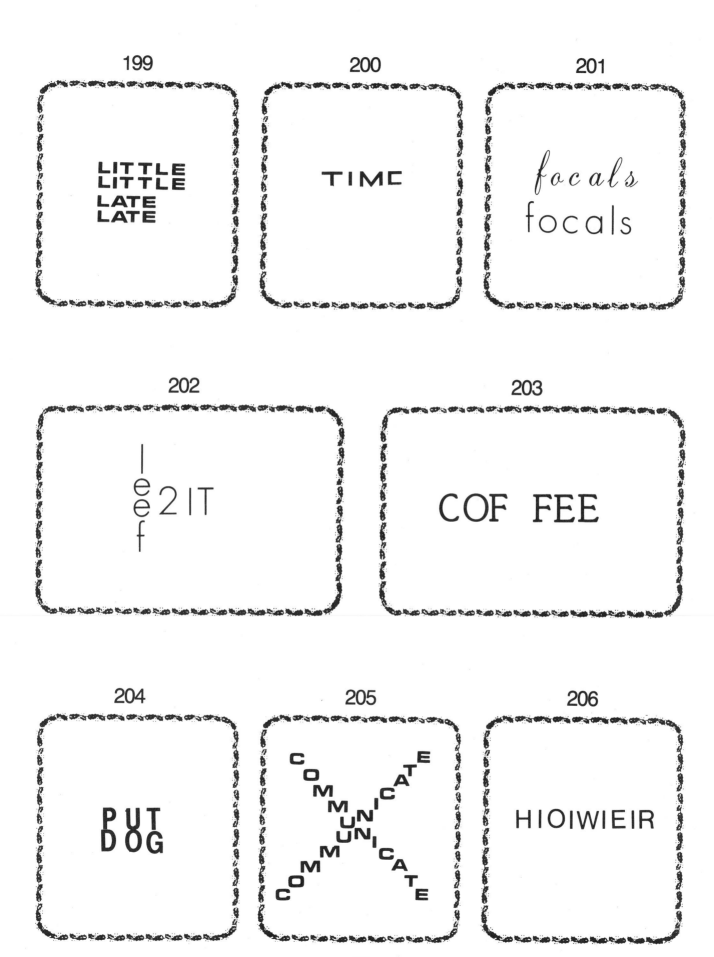

199

LITTLE
LITTLE
LATE
LATE

200

TIME

201

focals
focals

202

l
e
e 2 IT
f

203

COF FEE

204

PUT
DOG

205

COMMUNICATE
COMMUNICATE
COMMUNICATE
COMMUNICATE

206

HIOIWIEIR

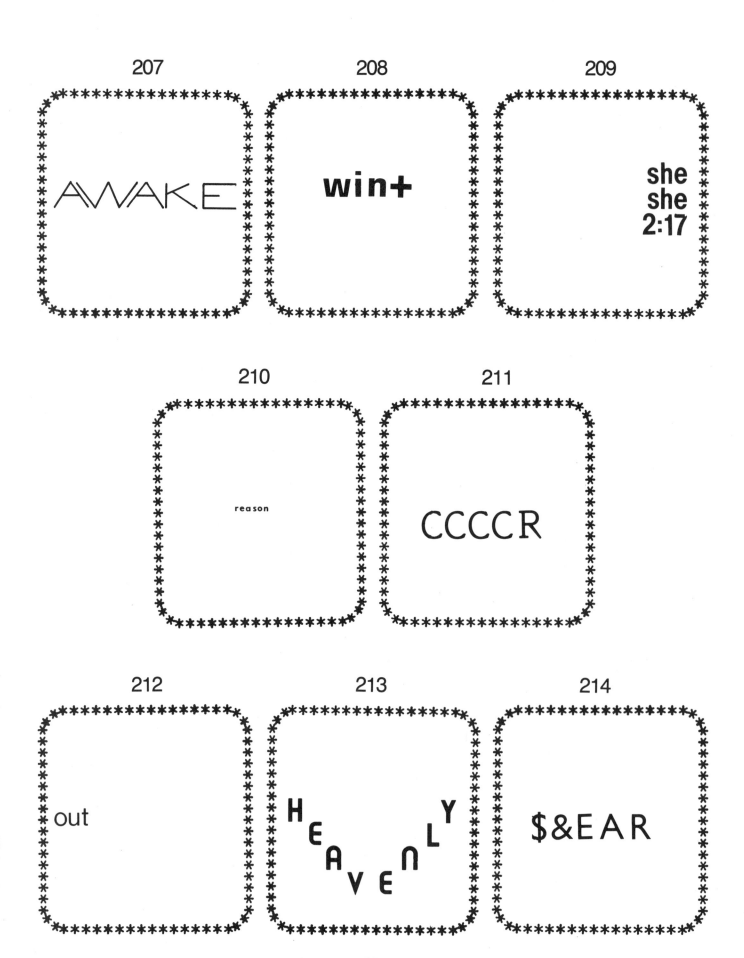

207

AWAKE

208

win+

209

she
she
2:17

210

reason

211

CCCCR

212

out

213

HEAVENLY

214

$&EAR

28

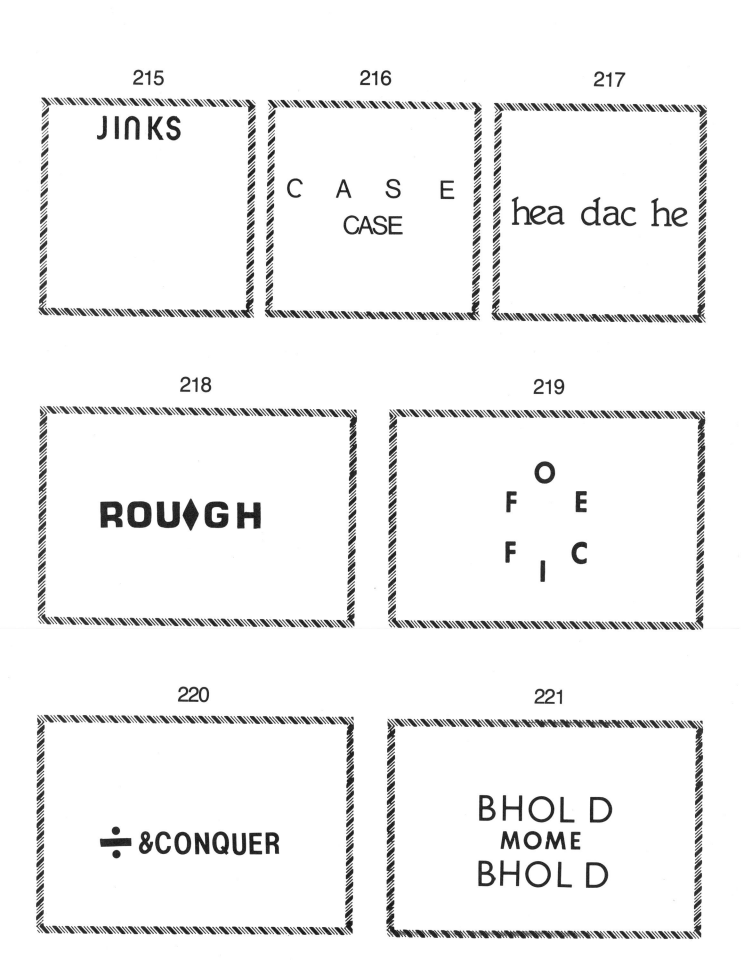

215

JINKS

216

C A S E
CASE

217

hea dac he

218

ROU◆GH

219

```
      O
F        E
  F   C
    I
```

220

÷ &CONQUER

221

BHOL D
MOME
BHOL D

222

+MARY

223

world

world

224

HAIRS

225

WHEREALL

226

e
l
k
c
u
b

safety
safety
safety
safety

227

10sshus

228

JONES JONES

229

¢¢OR

230

MIND

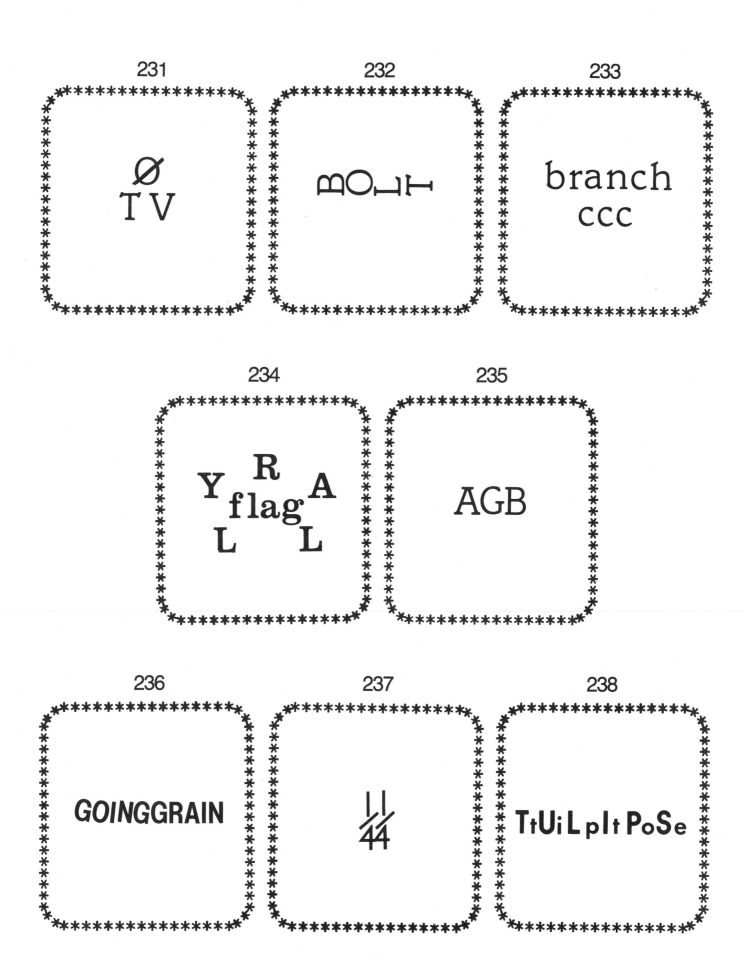

231

Ø
TV

232

BOLT

233

branch
ccc

234

Y R A
 flag
L   L

235

A̅GB

236

GOINGGRAIN

237

11/44

238

TtUiLpItPoSe

31

239

UP
HOUSE

240

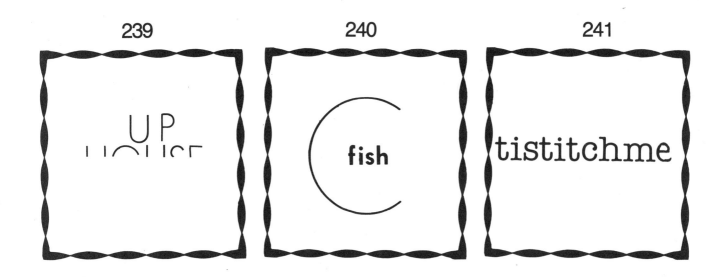

(fish

241

tistitchme

242

A
RM
F E

243

CO144ME

244

BITE

245

weather cast
cast
cast
cast

ANSWERS

Page 1

1. Death Valley
2. second to none
3. ageless
4. all in all
5. I'm counting on you.
6. The pen is mightier than the sword.
7. go down in history

Page 2

8. up for grabs
9. You win some and you lose some.
10. cracked ice
11. the calm before the storm
12. focal point
13. a piece of the action
14. stagger the imagination

Page 3

15. double agent
16. cross bow
17. 30 pounds overweight
18. belong
19. West Indies
20. About face!
21. buck up
22. big part in a small play

Page 4

23. Key West
24. wearing of the green
25. cross purposes
26. Frank Sinatra
27. barbell
28. reverse
29. full of anticipation
30. back to you

Page 5

31. biplane
32. bee in a bonnet
33. once upon a time
34. crisis in the family
35. brains over brawn
36. on the road again
37. going over the speed limit

Page 6

38. point blank
39. a flash in the pan
40. all seeing eye
41. adverb
42. Let bygones be bygones.
43. Too wise you are, too wise you be, I see you are too wise for me.
44. peas in a pod
45. Rocky Mountains
46. crushed ice

Page 7

47. a little bit more
48. hygiene
49. trouble in paradise
50. dead end
51. feeling under the weather
52. adding insult to injury
53. Spring ahead, Fall behind
54. a little behind in my work

Page 8

55. breakfast
56. dangerous undertow
57. forensic medicine
58. an eye for an eye, a tooth for a tooth
59. four-way stop
60. We Shall Overcome
61. better half